Nature Activities
Stargazing

by Ben Morgan

US Consultant Dr. Ted A. Maxwell, Associate Director for Collections
and Research, National Air & Space Museum, Smithsonian Institution
UK Consultant Dr. Jacqueline Mitton

LONDON, NEW YORK,
MELBOURNE, MUNICH, AND DELHI

Produced for Dorling Kindersley Ltd by
Cooling Brown Ltd:
Creative Director Arthur Brown
Editor Nikki Sims
Designers Tish Jones, Elly King,
Elaine Hewson, Mick Barratt
For Dorling Kindersley Ltd:
Senior Editors Fran Baines, Carey Scott
Senior Art Editor Stefan Podhorodecki
Managing Editor Linda Esposito
Managing Art Editor Jane Thomas
Publishing Managers Caroline Buckingham,
Andrew Macintyre
Jacket Designer Chris Drew
Jacket Copywriter/Editor Adam Powley,
Carrie Love
Art Director Simon Webb
Publishing Director Jonathan Metcalf
Production Controller Erica Rosen
Picture Researcher Liz Moore
DK Picture Library Sarah Mills
DTP Designer Natasha Lu
Photography Dave King

First American Edition, 2005
Published in the United States by
DK Publishing, Inc., 375 Hudson Street
New York, New York 10014

05 06 07 08 09   10 9 8 7 6 5 4 3 2

A Cataloging-in-Publication record for this book
is available from the Library of Congress.

ISBN 0-7566-1031-1

Color reproduction by Colourscan, Singapore
Printed in China by L. Rex Printing Co., Ltd.

Discover more at
www.dk.com

BE SAFE! IMPORTANT NOTE TO PARENTS

Some of the activities in this book require adult supervision.
Symbols are used to indicate where an activity must only be
done with the help of an adult. An "Important" box gives further
information about any risks involved and appropriate safety
precautions to take. Please carefully check which activities require
adult supervision and supervise your child where indicated.

 Activities shown with this symbol must only be
done with the help of an adult.

 Take extra care when doing this activity.

IMPORTANT
Provides safety
information and
indicates whether an
activity can be messy.
Follow the guidance
notes on those activities
that are messy and
should be carried out
only in suitable places.

Always ensure that your child follows
instructions carefully. The author and
the publisher will not be responsible
for any accident, injury, loss or damage
arising from any of the activities in this
book.

Contents

CHILDREN—BE SAFE!
READ THIS BEFORE STARTING ANY ACTIVITIES!

1 Tell an adult before you do any of the activities in this book, since you may need an adult to supervise the activity.

2 Pay attention to the following symbols:

⚠ Take extra care with an activity.

⚠ You need an adult to help you with an activity.

3 Read the "Important" boxes— these provide safety information and let you know which activities may be messy and should only be carried out in suitable places.

4 Follow the instructions carefully.

Stargazing

Have you ever looked at the night sky and
been amazed by all the stars? If so, this book
is for you. Stargazing is the world's oldest
hobby, and anyone can try it. It's not just
about learning constellations: you can see
galaxies and shooting stars, find planets in
the night sky, and watch an eclipse.

Where and when

The best time to stargaze is on a dark, clear night when there's no
moon. Winter nights are longer than those in the summer, but you
can stargaze year-round. What's more, you'll see different things at
different times of the year. You'll see more if you travel out of town,
since city lights create a hazy glow called "light pollution," which
blocks out all but the brightest stars. If you stargaze from home,
turn out the lights in your house and stand in the darkest spot in
your yard. Better still, visit the countryside or go on a camping trip.

Night vision

It takes about 20 minutes for your eyes to adjust to darkness. So
if you're patient and stay in the dark, you'll see more and more
stars. Don't look at bright light when your eyes have adjusted,
because you'll spoil your night vision. Some people use a red
flashlight for reading star charts and books because red light
doesn't interfere with your night vision. Another technique is
to close one eye when you're using a flashlight, so the other
remains as sensitive as possible.

*A planisphere (star chart)
shows which stars are
visible at different times
and dates*

USING THE INTERNET

The Internet is another exciting way to look at space. You can use it to see pictures taken by the world's best telescopes, or by spacecraft and rovers that are exploring the planets. Online planetarium websites can show you exactly which stars and planets are visible from where you live at any time. Astronomy news websites will give you information on forthcoming events to watch out for, such as meteor showers, eclipses, or passing comets.

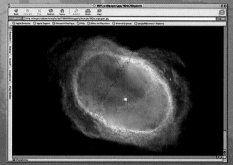

Planetary nebula
The latest pictures from the Hubble Telescope can be seen on the internet. This one shows the glowing shell of gas around a dying star.

Useful gear

The only essential equipment for stargazing is warm clothing—stargazers spend a lot of time standing or sitting still. A star chart (see pages 46-47) or astronomy book are useful if you want to find particular stars. To read them, you'll need a flashlight. A red light is best, since it will not affect your night vision. To make one, cover the end with a sheet of clear red plastic film. A compass, a watch, a notepad, and pen are also useful. Binoculars will help you to see small or faint objects much more clearly. Only expensive telescopes are significantly better than binoculars.

A sleeping bag will keep you warm

Keep books and papers off the ground, which may become wet with dew

HANDY TIP
A deck chair makes it much easier to look at the stars, since you won't have to lie on the ground.

The sky at night

The night sky can be very bewildering. There are thousands of stars, apparently sprinkled at random. To make matters worse, they are constantly moving around the sky. To help us make sense of the stars, we group them in patterns called constellations. To help us make sense of their movement, we imagine them being fixed to a giant moving globe that surrounds Earth.

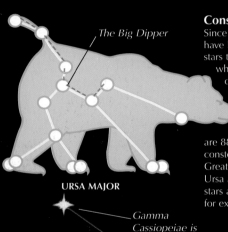

The Big Dipper

URSA MAJOR

Constellations

Since the earliest times, people have looked for patterns in the stars to help them remember which star is which. Many constellations were later given names from Roman and Greek myths, such as Orion (the Hunter) and Aries (the Ram). There are 88 internationally recognized constellations with Latin names. The Great Bear, for instance, is officially Ursa Major. Some well-known groups of stars are not constellations. The Big Dipper, for example, is part of the Great Bear.

South celestial pole

Gamma Cassiopeiae is 615 light-years away

Epsilon Cassiopeiae is 440 light-years away

Alpha Cassiopeiae is 230 light-years away

Beta Cassiopeiae is 54 light-years away

Delta Cassiopeiae is 100 light-years away from Earth

CASSIOPEIA

Just an illusion

Constellations are just the patterns we see from Earth. The stars that lie in the same direction appear to be in a group, but in reality they can be very far apart. Astronomers measure distances in space in light-years—1 light-year is the distance that light travels in a year (see page 9). The five stars making the "W" in Cassiopeia vary in distance from 54 light-years away to 615 light-years away.

North celestial pole

North Pole

Earth

Ecliptic

South Pole

Celestial equator

The celestial sphere

Stars move across the sky during the night much as the Sun does during the day. They move as though they were fixed points on a gigantic, rotating ball that surrounds the Earth. This ball doesn't really exist, but astronomers find it a useful concept and call it the "celestial sphere." The points of the sphere directly over Earth's North and South Poles, where the stars hardly move, are called celestial poles. Halfway between them is the "celestial equator." Every star has a fixed position on the celestial sphere and never shifts from that spot. In contrast, planets move against the starry background.

The yellow line—the ecliptic—is the Sun's apparent path across the celestial sphere

The orange line is the celestial equator. Stars here are visible in both the Northern and the Southern Hemispheres

MEASURING DISTANCE

Astronomers measure distances across the celestial sphere in degrees (°). The whole sphere covers 360°, but at night you can see only half the sphere (180°). You don't have to be a professional astronomer to measure distances; you can use your hand. Hold your hand at arm's length and use the guides shown on the right; these work no matter what age you are.

A finger's width
One finger is about 1° (twice the width of a full moon).

Half handspan
A closed hand at arm's length is about 10° across.

Whole handspan
An open hand with fingers fully splayed is about 22°.

Our place in space

For centuries, people thought that planet Earth was the center of the universe, with all the planets and stars revolving around us. With the invention of the telescope, astronomers started to realize that things were, in fact, quite different. Earth, as it turned out, is a small and insignificant planet orbiting just one of countless quadrillions of stars scattered across the vast cosmos.

Warmth from the Sun causes activity in the atmosphere, which affects the climate on Earth

Planet Earth and its star

Our planet is the only place in the universe known to support life. Earth is just the right distance from the Sun for water to be able to exist in all its forms: liquid water, solid ice, and water vapor. Water is essential for life. It covers two-thirds of the surface of Earth, and fills the sky with clouds. Our Sun is an average star. Its source of power is buried deep in the central core, where nuclear fusion reactions transform matter into energy. The Sun contains nearly all the matter in the solar system. It has tremendously powerful gravity, which keeps the planets trapped in orbit around it.

The planets

The Sun and planets make up the family of bodies that we call the solar system. There are at least nine planets orbiting the Sun, many with their own moons. The inner planets, including Earth, are made of rock and metal. Most of the outer planets are giant globes of hydrogen and helium, left over from the formation of the Sun. Beyond the gas giants lies tiny, icy Pluto. Between the outer and inner planets is a ring of rocky space debris, called the asteroid belt.

EXPLORING THE COSMOS

Distances in space are too big for the human mind to imagine. Astronomers measure them in light-years—1 light-year is the distance that light (the fastest thing in the universe) travels in one year, or 6 million million miles (10 million million km). The light we see from stars left them many years ago, and so we are looking back in time. With the world's most powerful telescopes, astronomers can see almost 14 billion light-years across space.

Scanning the skies
An amateur astronomer tries out the telescope at Kitt Peak Observatory. The observatory's domed roof opens to reveal the Milky Way.

The universe

Beyond the planets lies interstellar space, the darkness between the stars. If you traveled for long enough—about 500 years at the speed of a space shuttle—you would reach the Sun's nearest neighboring star, called Proxima Centauri. It is one of about 200 billion stars that make up our local galaxy, the Milky Way. Every star that you can see in the night sky belongs to this galaxy. Beyond the Milky Way are mind-bogglingly vast stretches of emptiness, and beyond these are yet more galaxies. There are probably hundreds of billions of galaxies stretching into the distance in all directions, but we will never know the exact number because we can only see a fraction of them. The galaxies and all the emptiness of space make up the universe.

Paper planets

Our solar system is made up of the Sun, nine planets, and at least 140 moons. Earth is one of the smaller planets, as you can see for yourself by making this mobile, which shows the planets' relative sizes. This mobile, however, doesn't include the Sun, which at this scale would be twice the height of your room!

WHAT YOU WILL NEED

- Pencil and compass
- Pushpin and string
- Thread
- 18 pieces of posterboard (ideally of nine colors)
- Ruler
- Scissors
- Pole 5 ft (1.5 m) long

Planet	Diameter
Mercury	1/2 in (1.5 cm)
Venus	11/2 in (4 cm)
Earth	11/2 in (4 cm)
Mars	3/4 in (2 cm)
Jupiter	181/2 in (47 cm)
Saturn	151/4 in (39 cm)
Uranus	61/4 in (16 cm)
Neptune	6 in (15 cm)
Pluto	1/2 in (1 cm)

Tie a pen to some string and mark half the diameter on it. Put a pin on the mark and push it into the center of the circle

1 **Use the pencil** and compass to draw circles on posterboard for the planets, following the measurements in the table. For the larger circles you will have to use a pushpin and string. Draw two circles for each planet.

2 **On each circle**, use the ruler to draw a straight line from the edge to the middle. Then cut along the length of that line (see picture below). Slot each pair of circles together.

Neptune

Pluto

3 **Make a pinhole** at the top of each planet and push some thread through. Loop the thread over the pole and tie on each planet in the order in the table. This mobile shows the order and the relative sizes of the planets but doesn't reveal how far apart they are. To make such a scale model, you would need a pole about 12 miles (20 km) long!

Jupiter

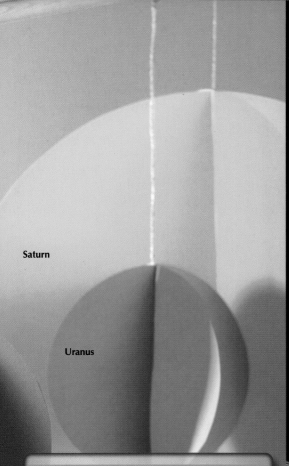

Saturn

Uranus

PLANETARY PROFILES

There are three kinds of planets. The four inner ones are rock and metal, the four giants are mostly liquid and gas, and Pluto is a mix of ice and rock.

Mercury ▶
A heavily cratered ball of rock and iron, Mercury scorches during the day but is freezing at night.

◀ Venus
Though similar in size and structure to Earth, Venus is baking hot and has poisonous, acidic air.

Earth ▶
Our home planet is the only place in the solar system known to have liquid water and life.

◀ Mars
Now a freezing, rust-covered desert, Mars almost certainly had liquid water in the past.

Jupiter ▶
By far the most massive planet, mighty Jupiter has no solid surface and more than 60 moons.

◀ Saturn
Saturn is a "lightweight" version of Jupiter, but with magnificent rings and blurry bands.

Uranus ▶
This blue-green giant has hazy clouds that are hard to see. Oddly, Uranus spins on its side.

◀ Neptune
Violent winds and gigantic storms whip across this giant's deep blue face.

Pluto ▶
This small ball of rock and ice is the largest of many icy bodies in the outer solar system.

BIRTH OF THE SOLAR SYSTEM

Our solar system formed 5 billion years ago in a vast, interstellar cloud of gas and dust. Part of the cloud began to shrink under its own gravity, and as it contracted it grew hotter and denser, and formed a spinning disk. The disk's core grew so dense and hot that it started shining, forming the Sun. Leftover debris clumped together to form planets and moons.

Formation of a planetary system around a star

Around and around

The planets travel around the Sun along paths called orbits. Their paths are not perfect circles but slightly squashed circles, called ellipses. Most planets have orbits that are only slightly elliptical, but that of Pluto, the outermost planet, is so elliptical that its orbit overlaps Neptune's. You can see how this happens by using loops of string to draw ellipses on a sheet of paper.

WHAT YOU WILL NEED

- Large sheet of paper (11 x 17 in or bigger)
- Large board that you can push tacks or small nails into
- Colored pins or tacks
- Ruler
- String
- Pens (one red, one blue)
- Scissors

AROUND THE SUN

Planets orbit the Sun because they are trying to move through space but are trapped by the powerful pull of the Sun's gravity. If you could turn the gravity off, the planets would speed away into space, traveling in straight lines. You can see how this works by tying a weight, such as a washer, to a string and swinging it around and around. The tight string is like the Sun's gravity. The weight would fly off if you let go of the string. If you stop whirling fast enough, the weight falls down. It is only because a planet is moving that it doesn't fall straight into the Sun.

Orbiting worlds ▲
Most of the planets orbit the Sun in roughly the same plane. There is one exception, however; Pluto's orbit (the farthest orbit at the back of the picture above) is tilted by about 10° from the rest.

Pluto's orbit is larger and more elliptical than Neptune's

Pluto's orbit

1 **Push two pins** into a large sheet of paper on an old table or a large board. Push the first pin into the middle of the paper— this pin represents the Sun. Push in the second pin exactly 3¹/4 in (8 cm) to the left of the first—this pin helps you draw the ellipse of Pluto's orbit.

2 **Now tie two loops** of string. The first loop should measure 5¹/2 in (14 cm) long when pulled straight. Tie the knot loosely at first, then hold the loop against the ruler and make small adjustments to the knot until the loop is exactly the right length; then pull tight. Repeat for the second loop but make this one 7¹/2 in (19 cm) long when pulled straight.

TRAPPED IN ORBIT

Satellites monitor the weather, transmit phone and TV signals, and take photographs of places and even people. The speed that a satellite travels depends on how close it is to Earth—the closer the satellite is, the faster it must fly to overcome Earth's gravity. A satellite in orbit 22,240 miles (35,790 km) above Earth takes 24 hours to circle the planet. Earth spins on its axis every 24 hours, so the satellite and planet move together and the satellite stays over the same spot.

A communications satellite

Pluto's orbit passes closer to the Sun at this point

Neptune's orbit

Reposition the pin to draw Neptune's orbit

Draw Pluto's orbit with the left pin here

Sun

HANDY TIP

Keep the tension on the string firm and even for the smoothest orbit paths.

3 **Place the longest loop** around the pins and hold a blue pen in the loop, pulling the string tight. Carefully draw around the pins, pulling on the string all the time and making sure it doesn't slip off. Label the blue ellipse "Pluto's orbit."

4 **Now reposition** the left pin so that it's only ½ in (1 cm) to the left of the other pin. Put the shorter loop around the tacks and use the red pen to draw another ellipse. Label this orbit "Neptune's orbit." Although Pluto orbits the Sun farther out than Neptune, you can see that its very elliptical orbit sometimes crosses Neptune's path and so passes closer to the Sun.

Seeing sunspots

The Sun is incredibly bright and you should never look at it directly. But you can create a safe image of it with binoculars and a cardboard screen. You can use this technique to watch planets pass in front of the Sun (transits), to see partial or total solar eclipses (see pages 18–19), and to search for sunspots.

Anchor the binoculars and support securely with books

WHAT YOU WILL NEED

- 2 sheets of cardboard
- Binoculars
- Scissors
- Paper
- Tape
- Pencil or pen

Don't look directly at the Sun and NEVER look at it through a telescope, binoculars, or even in a mirror.

WHAT ARE SUNSPOTS?

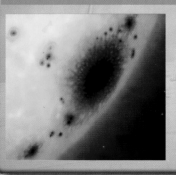

Sunspots are slightly darker, cooler patches on the Sun's surface. They might look small on the image made by your binoculars, but they are big enough to swallow Earth. By tracking sunspots over a period of time, astronomers discovered that the Sun doesn't rotate as a solid object. The poles take 35 days to rotate once, but the equator takes only 25 days.

◄ **Sunspots on the Sun's surface**

GREAT BALL OF FIRE?

The Sun isn't really a ball of fire but a gigantic globe of superhot hydrogen gas. Its power comes from its sheer weight. It contains 99.9 percent of all the matter in the solar system, and this huge mass crushes the core and forces atoms together in nuclear fusion reactions. The energy escapes as heat, light, radiation, and violent eruptions from the surface.

Sun storm ▶
A loop of superhot gas erupts from the Sun. Storms like this are most frequent during a "solar maximum" – a period every 11 years when sunspot numbers reach a peak.

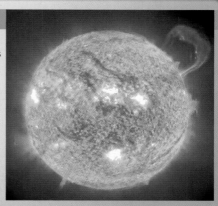

Sun's rays

1 **Make a shield** to hold the binoculars using cardboard and scissors. To allow sunlight through one lens only, cover the other lens with cardboard or a lens cap. Prop the shield with the binoculars on a chair so they face the Sun directly and secure them.

2 **Place the other piece** of cardboard in the shadow of the binoculars, about 3 ft (1 m) away, to act as a screen. Tilt the binoculars until an image of the Sun appears on the screen. Sharpen the image by focusing the binoculars.

3 **Look for dark sunspots** in the image. Tape some paper on to the screen and trace the Sun and any sunspots. Repeat the next day and look for the same sunspots—they will have shifted as the Sun turns.

Angle the screen so that it's facing the binoculars

What time is it?

Earth turns around once every 24 hours, and this is why the Sun appears to cross the sky and vanish over the horizon, creating our day and night. Earth's rotation is so regular that you can use the Sun to tell time. The best way to do this is to build a sundial, a device that was first used around 6,000 years ago.

WHAT YOU WILL NEED

- Pencil
- Block of wood
- Ruler
- Protractor
- Permanent marker pen
- Atlas
- Small piece of thin wood
- Plasticine/modeling clay
- Craft glue
- Compass

Ask an adult to help to construct a solid base.

Use a compass to be sure your sundial faces in the right direction

Setting up your sundial

Take the sundial outside and place it on a flat surface. Point the pencil north if you live in the Northern Hemisphere or south if you live in the Southern Hemisphere. If your country adjusts clocks according to the season, the time may be an hour or more off.

Solid wooden base

Hour markers

1 **Draw a straight line** across the board 1–2 in (2.5–5 cm) from one end and mark its center with a dot. Use the protractor to draw rays 15° apart from this point; draw these rays in pencil first in case you make any mistakes. When you've finished, use the permanent marker pen to draw over the pencil lines and write the times as shown (above right). If your base is circular, start from the center of the board and draw rays all around, as on a clock face.

15°

EARLY TIMEKEEPERS

About 6,000 years ago, people in the Middle East began using shadows to tell time, and so invented sundials—the world's first clocks. Sundials were popular for centuries, but since they work only when it's sunny, inventors came up with other clock ideas, including notched candles and pendulums. It was only about 150 years ago that mechanical clocks became watch-sized.

Wooden sundial ▶
Some sundials had a compass built into their design for quick and easy time-telling.

In the Northern Hemisphere, this end of the pencil should point north—in the Southern Hemisphere, it should point south

Built-in compass

Angle here must match your latitude

6 pm

4 pm

3 pm

6 am

7 am

8 am

9 am

12 noon

11 am

10 am

HANDY TIP

To weatherproof your sundial, ask an adult to paint it with clear wood varnish.

(2) The part of the sundial that casts a shadow is called the "gnomon." The angle under the gnomon must be the same as your latitude (see pages 56–57 for more about latitude). Use an atlas to find out your latitude. Then, ask an adult to cut the small piece of wood into a triangle, with one corner cut to the angle of your latitude.

(3) Use the Plasticine or modeling clay to fix the pencil to the dot in the middle of the line at the end of the board. Position the triangle under the pencil, making sure that the corner matching your latitude is in the Plasticine. Adjust until it all fits snugly, then glue the triangle in place and let the glue set.

When darkness comes

One of the most amazing astronomical events you can ever see is a total solar eclipse, when the Moon passes in front of the Sun. During a total eclipse, the Sun is blocked by the Moon and twilight falls on Earth. During a partial eclipse, the Moon just takes a "bite" out of the Sun.

Diamond ring
Just before and after the Moon covers the Sun during a total solar eclipse, the rays of sunlight may shine through valleys on the Moon, creating a beautiful "diamond ring" effect.

How it works
A solar eclipse occurs when the Moon comes directly between the Sun and Earth, blocking out the sunlight and casting a shadow on Earth. The shadow has two parts: the umbra and the penumbra. The umbra is the darkest part of the shadow, where all sunlight is blocked; this is where total eclipses occur. In the penumbra, the Sun is only partly blocked; this is where partial eclipses occur. Partial eclipses are much more common than total eclipses, but less spectacular.

Moon

The inner, darker part of the Moon's shadow (the umbra)

Watch an eclipse safely
Never look directly at the Sun without eye protection officially approved as safe. Sunglasses or homemade filters do not protect your eyes enough. During a total eclipse, it is safe to remove goggles briefly during totality, when the Sun is completely blocked. Do not try to view a partial eclipse, the partial stage of a total eclipse, or the diamond-ring stage with the naked eye.

The early stages of a total eclipse

Totality

A total eclipse occurs only in the central part of the Moon's shadow

IMPORTANT
Don't look directly at the Sun, and NEVER look at it through a telescope, binoculars, or via a mirror.

The outer part of the Moon's shadow (the penumbra) covers a much wider area

Earth

WATCHING A PARTIAL ECLIPSE

The best way to see a partial eclipse is to make a device called a pinhole camera, which creates an image of the Sun. Cut a small circular hole in one end of a shoe box and tape some aluminum foil over the hole. Then, use a compass to make a pin-hole in the foil. At the other end of the box, cut out a square and tape tracing paper over the square to make a screen. During the eclipse, point the pinhole end of the box toward the Sun, and watch the image appear safely on the paper screen.

Hold the box toward the Sun

Watch the screen

Light enters through the pin-hole at one end of the box

Lunar landscape

The Moon is the closest heavenly body to Earth and the easiest to see. Even with the naked eye you can see the dark lunar "seas" and brighter highlands, but with binoculars or a telescope you can also see a wealth of craters, mountains, and other features.

The mountains around Mare Imbrium and Serenitatis are the remains of vast crater rims

SCARFACE

The Moon's highlands are covered with craters made by meteorite collisions, but the darker "seas" have few craters. Astronomers think most of the craters formed early in the Moon's history. Earth was battered by meteorites at the same time, but our craters have since been worn away by weather and geological forces. After the bombardment ended, molten lava oozed from the Moon's interior and spread across the lowlands, wiping out some craters and forming the lunar seas, or maria.

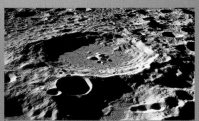

A large lunar crater with central hills

Oceanus Procellarum (Ocean of Storms)

Mare Humorum (Sea of Moisture)

The Ocean of Storms is the largest of the Moon's maria

When to observe the Moon

A full moon is not the best time to view the Moon. All other times are better because the Sun's sideways illumination casts shadows from lunar mountains and crater rims, making them stand out more. The Moon's features are most clear at the "terminator"—the border between the lit and the unlit area. The terminator sweeps across the Moon over the course of a month (see pages 22–23), making different features stand out at different times.

Lunar seas are large, level basalt plains on the Moon's surface

Plato crater

Mare Imbrium
(Sea of Rains)

MAKING CRATERS

The Moon has been pounded by so
many meteorites that many of the
craters overlap or formed on top
of older craters. You can create
a similar effect with a tray of
sand and "meteorites" of
varying sizes, such as balls and
marbles. Flatten the sand, then drop
the meteorites from overhead.

Homemade craters

Mare Serenitatis
(Sea of Serenity)

Mare
Crisium
(Sea of
Crises)

Copernicus crater

Mare Tranquillitatis
(Sea of Tranquillity)

Mare
Fecunditatis
(Sea of
Fertility)

Theophilus crater ▶

Mare
Nectaris
(Sea of
Nectar)

*Apollo 11
landing site
where people
first stood on
the Moon*

Mare
Nubium
(Sea of
Clouds)

Tycho crater

*The bright rays around Tycho are vast
streaks of debris thrown out by the
meteorite impact that formed the crater.
These are best seen during a full moon*

A lunar calendar

Unlike the Sun, the Moon doesn't make
light of its own. Instead, we see the Moon
in the sky only when it reflects light from
the Sun—it acts like an enormous mirror.
As the Moon travels around Earth on its
monthly orbit, we see it at different
angles relative to the Sun. It changes from
a thin crescent to a full disk, passing
through a series of stages called phases.
If you watch the Moon every day
for a month, you can record
the whole cycle of phases.

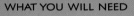

WHAT YOU WILL NEED

- Pen
- Sheet of white paper
- Compass
- Sheet of black paper
- Scissors
- Glue
- Aluminum foil
- Binoculars

1 **Draw a chart** with 29
squares, made of four
rows of seven squares and one
extra square (see right). Cut out
29 circles from the black paper
and stick one in each square.

Write the
numbers 1 to 29
in the squares

2 **Wait for a clear night** when you
can see the Moon. Binoculars might
help you check the Moon's shape, but they
aren't essential. Cut out its shape to match
in aluminum foil and glue it onto the first
black circle of the chart.

3 **Do the same** every day for a month.
To find out when the Moon rises and
sets each day, look in a newspaper. Some
nights will be cloudy, so leave those blank.

THE PHASES OF THE MOON

At new moon, the Moon is between the Earth and the Sun. It crosses the sky during daylight hours, but we don't see it because it's hidden by the Sun's glare, and only its far side is sunlit. Over the next days, the Moon moves away from the Sun in the sky and sunlight spills around its edge, forming a crescent that is easiest to see after sunset. When half the Moon's face is lit, it is a quarter of the way through its orbit (first quarter), and at this stage is visible from noon to midnight. As the sunlit area grows (waxes), we see the Moon more at night. When it is halfway through its orbit, it is opposite the Sun and fully lit in the night sky—then, we see it as a full moon.

The changing face of the Moon

Full Moon

Waning Gibbous

Waxing Gibbous

Last Quarter

First Quarter

Waning Crescent

New Moon
(not visible from Earth)

Waxing Crescent

Moon detective

If you have binoculars, take a close look at the Moon each day. You'll see different features as the month progresses and the angle of sunlight striking the Moon changes. The best place to look is near the terminator—the dividing line between the areas of shadow and light.

Aluminum foil

Moon shadows

A lunar eclipse takes place when the Moon passes through Earth's shadow. This happens perhaps once or twice a year, but it's always worth watching because each eclipse is different. Lunar eclipses are also safe to watch and easy to see—you can watch one from anywhere with a view of the Moon.

Moon in penumbra

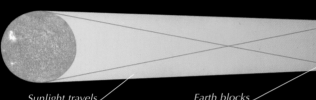

Umbra

Penumbra

Sunlight travels from the Sun toward Earth

Earth blocks the light and casts a shadow

An eclipse happens when the Moon enters the umbra

How it works ▲

Lunar eclipses can happen only at a full moon, when the Moon is on the opposite side of Earth from the Sun and comes close to Earth's shadow. Earth's shadow has two parts: an outer zone called the penumbra, where sunlight is reduced; and an inner zone called the umbra, where all direct sunlight is blocked. A total eclipse is when the whole Moon enters the umbra. If only part of the Moon enters the umbra, it is a partial eclipse.

◄ Viewing an eclipse

You don't need special equipment to watch an eclipse, but binoculars or a good-quality telescope allow you to see extra details. Total lunar eclipses are the most interesting but they don't happen every year. To find out when the next one is due and where you can see it, look up lunar eclipses on the Internet.

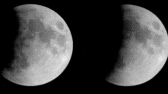

Moon entering umbra

Moon approaching totality

Stages of an eclipse

The main eclipse begins when the Moon first enters the umbra. A dark shadow appears in the side of the Moon and slowly creeps across it over the next hour or so. At the same time, moonlight fades and the sky darkens. The Moon looks different from a normal crescent at this stage because the shadow is much less curved and lacks a crisp edge. When the shadow covers the Moon entirely, the Moon is totally eclipsed but still faintly visible. Totality lasts anything up to 1 hour 47 minutes. Afterward, the earlier stages of the eclipse are repeated, but in reverse.

WHY DOESN'T THE MOON DISAPPEAR?

Try this activity to find out why the Moon doesn't disappear completely during an eclipse. Line up a ball, a globe, and a desk lamp in a dark room. Imagine that the globe is Earth and the ball is the Moon. Switch on the light and place the ball in Earth's shadow. Now, mix an "atmosphere" for Earth: add a teaspoon of milk to a clear plastic bottle and fill with water. Hold the bottle on top of the globe and watch the Moon. The milky water scatters light, casting a pinkish glow on the Moon even though it's in Earth's shadow.

The ball represents the Moon

The milky water represents Earth's atmosphere

The globe blocks the light, casting a shadow

Desk lamp

Totality

The most spectacular part of a lunar eclipse is totality, when the Moon is completely within the umbra. Sunlight scattered by Earth's atmosphere can turn the Moon copper red during totality. It's also the time when stars are brightest and the Milky Way may become more visible.

Escape velocity

The faster an object moves, the harder it is to stop. This principle governs the movement of planets, moons, stars, and spacecraft, which hurtle through space at terrific speed but are pulled toward each other by gravity. With bearings and a magnet, you can investigate how speed (velocity) can help objects escape the forces pulling them.

WHAT YOU WILL NEED

- Scissors
- An old cereal box
- Book
- Plasticine/modeling clay
- Flat magnet
- Steel ball bearings
- Large magnet

1 **Cut a strip of cardboard** 12 in long by 3 in wide (30 cm by 6 cm) from a cereal box and fold it into a V-shape.

2 **Raise one end** on a book and fix it to a piece of Plasticine or modeling clay to form a long ramp. Place a flat magnet under the other end of the ramp.

3 **Roll steel bearings** down the ramp. Start from a low position on the ramp and see if they roll past the magnet or stick to it. Then try higher positions and see if they roll over the magnet without sticking. Adjust the steepness of the ramp if they always stick or never stick.

The speed of the bearing determines whether or not it sticks to the magnet or escapes its magnetic field

THE PULL OF GRAVITY

Gravity is an invisible force that pulls all objects in the universe together. Massive objects, like planets, have powerful gravity. Their gravity works like the magnet in this experiment, capturing objects that fly past. Slow-moving objects are pulled in so powerfully that they crash into the surface, or end up trapped in orbit as moons. Fast-moving objects hurtle past and are not trapped, although the force of gravity might deflect their path, or even speed them up.

◄ **Deep impact**
A massive asteroid succumbs to gravity and crashes into Earth in this artist's impression. A collision like this may have wiped out the dinosaurs.

Adjust the angle of the ramp to control the speed of the bearings

HANDY TIP

Turn the magnet lengthwise if the bearings roll past too easily.

Upturned magnet

4 **Remove the flat magnet** and see where a bearing will roll without anything in its way. Then place a powerful magnet near the end of the ramp, but to one side. Try again and see how the magnetic force bends the bearing's path. You may need to keep adjusting the magnet's position until it has a noticeable effect without trapping the bearing.

Use a powerful magnet to deflect the path of the bearings

UP, UP AND AWAY!

Just as the bearings in this experiment had to reach a certain speed to escape the magnet, spacecraft must reach a certain speed—called escape velocity—to escape the pull of Earth's gravity. Escape velocity at Earth's surface is 25,000 mph (40,000 km/h). Anything traveling upward at a slower speed than this will fall back down. It takes powerful rockets to accelerate spacecraft to reach escape velocity. But most rockets usually aim only to reach orbital velocity—the speed at which satellites and other cargo become trapped in orbit around Earth.

Ariane 5 ▶
The European rocket Ariane 5 is equipped with two side boosters and two main rocket stages. All are needed to carry space probes fast enough to escape Earth's pull.

Ready for liftoff

Rockets are launched into space by the hot gases from the burning fuel rushing backward out of their engines. In just the same way, a balloon will fly through the air if you let the gas inside it escape. If you use two balloons, as here, you can make a simple model of a two-stage rocket.

WHAT YOU WILL NEED

- Plastic cup
- Scissors
- 1 long balloon
- 1 round balloon
- Adhesive tape or a paperclip

ROCKET STAGES

When ready for liftoff, a rocket can weigh thousands of tons, and almost all of that is due to the fuel on board. It takes immense power to lift such a huge weight off the ground and propel it all the way up into space. To make the job easier, rockets are divided into a series of two or three stages, stacked on top of each other. When each stage has used up its fuel, it falls away to lighten the load, making the job of the next stage easier. Only the tip of the rocket makes it all the way into space.

◄ **Separation**
When each stage is spent, explosive charges separate it from the rocket. This explosion prompts boosters to ignite in the next stage.

Point the rocket upward before you launch it

If you need help, ask an adult to cut the bottom off the cup

1 **Carefully cut** the bottom out of a large plastic or paper cup. Partially inflate a long balloon and pull the open end through the bottom of the cup.

Use the longest balloon you can get

2 **Blow more air** into the long balloon but don't fully inflate it. Fold the end over the bottom of the cup and tape it in place.

ROCKETS OF THE FUTURE

Rockets carry two fuels: liquid hydrogen and liquid oxygen. Hundreds of tons of both are needed, which not only makes rockets heavy but also makes launches incredibly expensive. To cut costs, engineers are designing rockets that work like jet engines, sucking in oxygen from the air rather than carrying it on board. Such "air-breathing" craft would be lighter and more maneuverable than current rockets or space shuttles. They might even carry tourists on short trips to space.

Space express ▲
This artist's impression shows one design for an air-breathing rocket to replace the space shuttle.

HANDY TIP
Tape a straw to the long balloon and guide the rocket along some fishing line.

The long balloon forms the second stage of this rocket

The small, first-stage balloon keeps the end of the long balloon closed

Temporarily tape the end of the long balloon

3 **Push the round balloon** into the bottom of the cup and inflate it so it holds the first balloon closed. Remove the tape holding the long balloon. Now, release the balloon and see how far the rocket travels.

Finding Venus

The lone bright star that often appears in the evening as the Sun goes down is not a star at all, but the planet Venus. Venus is the closest planet to Earth, and the brightest object in the night sky after the Moon. Sunlight reflected from its dense clouds can make Venus 15 times brighter than the brightest star.

EARTH'S NON-IDENTICAL TWIN

Of all the planets, Venus is most like Earth. It's about the same size, has a similar composition, and has a cloudy atmosphere. But, unlike Earth, Venus is a roasting, waterless desert, far too hot for life—the surface temperature is 900°F (480°C). One reason for the extreme heat on Venus is that it's closer to the Sun. Another reason is that its dense atmosphere is full of carbon dioxide gas, which traps heat by the "greenhouse effect."

◀ Through the clouds
Clouds cover Venus, but radar cameras can see through. This image reveals volcanoes, twisting valleys, and ancient lava flows.

1 **Go outside** on a clear evening just after sunset and look West, toward the sunset. Alternatively, go out just before dawn and look East. If you can see a single, very bright "star" that doesn't twinkle, it's probably Venus. Venus is always close to the Sun, so as the sky darkens and the Sun sinks deeper beyond the horizon, Venus will set, too.

Venus

Moon

ON THE SURFACE

Some call Venus the "closest thing to hell in the solar system." The clouds are made of deadly sulfuric acid, the air is hot enough to melt lead, and the air pressure is 90 times that on Earth. If you landed there, you'd be poisoned, roasted, and crushed to death in seconds. The few spacecraft that have landed on Venus lasted only minutes before the lethal conditions destroyed them.

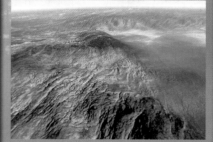

Venusian mountains ▲
Scientists used radar data to create this 3-D view across the highlands of Venus. Some of the mountains might be volcanoes.

2 **Look at Venus** with binoculars. You won't see any surface details because the planet is covered with thick clouds. But sometimes you can see a crescent shape formed by the pattern of sunlight and shade on the planet (just as the Moon sometimes forms a crescent). Venus looks biggest when it's a crescent, and smallest when it's full because of the way we see it during its orbit.

Going through phases

Venus' appearance changes as it orbits the Sun. As it approaches its closest point to Earth, we see a large crescent Venus. As it reaches its farthest point from Earth, we see a small disk. Halfway between these points we see a semicircle, and when Venus lines up exactly with the Sun, we don't see it at all because it is lost in the Sun's glare.

Crescent Venus

Sun

Earth

Why is Mars red?

The Greeks named the planet Mars after a god of war because its color reminded them of blood. The color is easy to see with the naked eye when Mars passes close to Earth, though it's more of an orangey-brown than a red. The cause, as you can find out for yourself, is a very familiar substance: rust, or iron oxide.

WHAT YOU WILL NEED

- Sand
- Tray
- Rubber gloves
- Scissors
- Steel wool
- Pitcher of salty water (1 teaspoon of salt to 2 or 3 cups of water)

In 1997, the Sojourner *rover landed on Mars and studied chemicals in the rocks*

Iron oxide in the dust on Mars gives the planet its color

SIGNS OF WATER?

Three billion years ago, water may have flowed on Mars. There may have been shallow oceans, a thick atmosphere, and life. Today, Mars is a bitterly cold desert, with air so thin that liquid water would vaporize in seconds. Even so, there is tantalizing evidence that water still exists, perhaps in a frozen form deep underground or trapped in Mars's polar ice caps. Space probes have photographed freshly eroded gullies on Mars, in places like Newton Basin. Perhaps such features formed when underground ice reserves thawed and seeped to the surface.

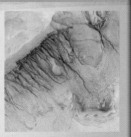

Newton Basin

1 **Place a layer of sand** on the bottom of a tray. Put on the rubber gloves and use the scissors to snip steel wool into small bits across the sand. Try to pull the bits apart to stop the steel wool from clumping and to help spread it out through the sand. While wearing the gloves, mix it well into the sand with your hands.

THE RED PLANET

Scientists are not sure how the iron oxide on Mars formed. On Earth, rust forms when iron reacts with the oxygen in air, a process that is much faster when water is present. But Mars has no liquid water on the surface and its air is almost oxygen-free. Some experts think the iron oxide formed long ago when iron in Martian rocks reacted with water in ancient rivers and seas. Another theory is that the iron built up from tiny meteorites raining onto the surface.

Martian weather ▶
The Hubble telescope took this picture of Mars. It shows an ice cap at its south pole, swirling clouds of ice in the north, and a dust storm in the southeast.

HANDY TIP
Stir the sand around each day to create an even color.

(2) Pour the salty water on the sand to wet it, but without covering it completely. Leave the tray where it won't be disturbed for a few days.

(3) Check the tray daily and add water if it dries out. The sand will slowly turn rusty red—like Martian soil.

Is there life on Mars?

In 1976, scientists sent two spacecraft—the *Viking* landers—to Mars to test the dusty soil for signs of microscopic organisms. This activity mimics one of the tests, using sand instead of Martian soil. First, you add nutrients to the sand, then you wait for a reaction. Chemicals in the sand may react quickly but briefly. Living cells (such as yeast) will react slowly but increasingly as they feed and multiply.

WHAT YOU WILL NEED

- Three jars
- Clean, dry sand
- Three colored labels
- Three teaspoons
- Salt
- Baking powder
- Dried yeast
- Warm water
- Sugar
- Glass jug
- Vinegar

HANDY TIP

This experiment can make a mess, so stand your jars on a tray or old newspaper.

Nothing happens in the red jar

The sand and salt are thoroughly mixed

Sand with added salt

1 **Half-fill three jars** with dry (or fairly dry) sand and stick different-colored labels on them. Using different teaspoons (to prevent contamination), add 2 teaspoons of salt to the red jar, 2 teaspoons of baking powder to the yellow jar, and 2 teaspoons of yeast to the blue jar. Give each jar a stir or shake (with the lid on or a hand over the top) to mix the powder and sand thoroughly.

2 **Pour two cups** of warm water into the glass pitcher. Add half a cup of sugar and, once dissolved, add 2 teaspoons of vinegar.

3 **Carefully pour** an equal amount of sugar water into each jar. Don't pour it suddenly or it could produce froth and ruin the experiment. Is there an immediate reaction in any of the jars?

SEARCHING FOR SIGNS OF LIFE

The *Viking* landers found no clear evidence of life on Mars, but the hunt goes on. Astronomers are now fairly sure that Mars once had (and may still have) liquid water, which is a vital ingredient for life. In 1996 scientists found what looked like fossilized microbes in a Martian meteorite. No tests for life have been carried out on Mars yet, but new probes are now in development.

Spirit rover ▶
In 2004, this robotic buggy landed on Mars and found plenty of evidence that Mars once had water. Future rovers will carry out tests for life.

A slow, dramatic reaction happens in the blue jar as yeast cells feed on the sugar and multiply

There is a brief chemical reaction in the yellow jar as the baking powder reacts with the vinegar

Sand with added baking powder

4 **Take a look** after 1 hour, and then again after 2 hours. What kind of reaction would you expect if there were living organisms present?

Sand with added yeast

Stormy weather

Gigantic Jupiter is the largest planet of all—more than twice the mass of all the other planets combined. It is a colossal ball of liquid covered with swirling gases. Its ferocious winds and storms stir the gases into colorful stripes and whirlpools. You can create a very similar effect with milk and food coloring.

WHAT YOU WILL NEED

- Large bowl
- Whole milk
- Teaspoon
- Red and yellow food coloring
- Dishwashing liquid

Spots and stripes

In Jupiter's freezing upper atmosphere, the gases have condensed into striped clouds colored by a cocktail of chemicals. Spots and ovals are storms. Jupiter's Great Red Spot is a hurricane, twice the size of Earth, that has been raging for 300 years.

HANDY TIP

Rest the bowl on the table as you turn it so that it moves gently and smoothly.

The food coloring floats on the surface of the milk

Great Red Spot

Swirly patterns form as the liquids rotate

1 Carefully pour half a mug of whole milk into a large mixing bowl. Pour it down the side of the bowl so it doesn't splash and form bubbles on the surface. Let it stand for a minute until the milk is still.

2 With great care, use a teaspoon to add a big drop of each food coloring to the surface of the milk. Do this by touching the milk gently with the spoon, and don't stir.

3 Turn the bowl around gently so that the milk and food coloring start to swirl, like the colored clouds in Jupiter's storms. It takes some practice to get a really good storm. Experiment with different amounts of food coloring, and be careful not to swirl the bowl too quickly.

Voyager spacecraft

Exploring Jupiter

Astronauts could never visit Jupiter because the planet is surrounded by deadly radiation and has no solid surface to land on. Five robotic space probes have made trips there, among them *Voyager 1* and *2* in 1979, which sent back more than 33,000 photos as well as a film of clouds swirling around the Great Red Spot.

SUICIDE PROBE

In 1995, a coffee-table-sized package parachuted into Jupiter's clouds to study the planet's stormy weather. The *Galileo* probe hit Jupiter at 115,000 mph (185,000 km/h) but soon slowed down in the "thick" air. Its canopy opened, and the probe spent nearly an hour measuring the wind and analyzing chemicals before heat destroyed it.

◄ The *Galileo* probe

4 **To kick up** a really violent storm, add a single drop of dishwashing liquid. This will disperse the colors quickly by helping the food coloring dissolve.

Jupiter and its moons

Jupiter is one of the brightest planets you can see from Earth. Through good binoculars you can see its rounded shape and its four largest moons. With a telescope, you can even see its stripes.

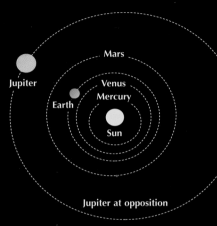

Jupiter at opposition

1 **Find out** when Jupiter is at "opposition"—that is, when Jupiter's orbit brings it closest to Earth and on exactly the opposite side of Earth from the Sun, making Jupiter visible all night. You can see Jupiter easily for weeks before, and after, opposition. In the period after opposition, Jupiter is high in the evening sky, so it's easy to see without staying up late.

Dates when Jupiter is at opposition	Constellation it appears in
April 3, 2005	Virgo
May 4, 2006	Libra
June 6, 2007	Ophiuchus
July 9, 2008	Sagittarius
August 14, 2009	Capricornus
September 21, 2010	Pisces
October 29, 2011	Aries
December 3, 2012	Taurus
January 5, 2014	Gemini

Lining up

Sometimes several planets line up—an event known as "alignment." This picture shows an alignment of Jupiter (left), Mars (middle), and Venus (right). Planets never align perfectly because their orbits don't lie in exactly the same plane.

HANDY TIP

Jupiter and other planets are easy to tell apart from stars because they don't twinkle.

2 **Search for Jupiter** in the month before, or after, opposition. Go out on a clear night and use a compass to face South if you live in the Northern Hemisphere, or North if you live in the Southern Hemisphere. Using a planisphere (see pages 44–45), locate the constellation listed in the table on the left, then look in that constellation for an unusually bright and yellowish "star" that doesn't twinkle—that's Jupiter.

WHAT YOU WILL NEED

- Compass
- Planisphere
- Binoculars

FOUR OF A KIND

At least 60 moons orbit Jupiter, trapped in the massive planet's powerful gravity. Many are captured asteroids, but several are so big that we'd call them planets if they orbited the Sun. The four largest are called the Galilean moons, after the Italian astronomer Galileo. Their order from Jupiter is Io, Europa, Ganymede then Callisto, and the closer they are to Jupiter, the more active they are. Below they are shown in order of size, smallest first.

Europa ▶
Sheets of ice cover this moon, but there may be an ocean of liquid water deep beneath. Some scientists think primitive life forms might live in this hidden ocean.

Io ▶
The most volcanically active object in the solar system, Io has more than 100 volcanoes spewing sulfur and gas far out into space. The volcanic activity leads to changes in Io's surface color.

Callisto ▶
Billions of years ago, meteorites rained down on this moon and peppered its surface with craters. Since then, Callisto seems to have barely changed. Like Europa, this moon may have a subsurface ocean, but the evidence for this is uncertain.

Ganymede ▶
The largest Galilean moon is Ganymede. This world is a mixture of rock and ice, with white scars where swirling forces inside the moon have cracked the surface. Ganymede has mountains, valleys, and solidified lava flows.

You can see the four largest moons via binoculars as pinpricks of light. Look again on a different night to see how their patterns change

3 **Look at Jupiter** with binoculars. Rest your elbows on a firm surface to steady your view. Can you see Jupiter's four largest moons? If any are missing, they may be in front of, or behind, Jupiter.

Saturn's strange shape

Saturn is nearly ten times wider than Earth,
yet it spins more than twice as fast. It rotates
so quickly that its equator bulges outward,
making Saturn the flattest planet in our
solar system. The force that creates the
bulge is called centrifugal
force, and you can see it for
yourself by making a
spinning paper model.

WHAT YOU WILL NEED

- Scissors
- 8½-by-11-in paper in
  two colors
- Ruler
- Bamboo skewer
- Adhesive tape
- Drinking straw
- Long rubber band
- Key ring or similar ring
- Plasticine/modeling clay
- Pencil

In a spin
Saturn rotates once every 10 hours
39 minutes, its equator whizzing
around at a dizzying 22,000 mph
(35,000 km/h). As a result,
Saturn is about 10 percent
wider than it is tall.

*Centrifugal force
pushes the paper
strips, making them
curve outward in
the middle*

*Make sure the
strips are
evenly spaced*

1 **Cut the end** off two sheets of letter-
sized colored paper so that they are
about 2 in (5 cm) shorter than your skewer.
Then cut the paper into long thin strips, each
about ¼ in (0.5 cm) long. Neatly lay about
20 strips, alternating the colors, flat on a
table. Place a length of tape across
each end of the strips to stick to
them all at once (see above). Now lift
up the entire sheet, being careful not to
lose any of the strips, and flip it over.

*Second
piece of
straw*

*Allow enough
tape to stick to
the straws*

2 **Add another two lengths** of tape at
the edges only this time, allowing extra at
each end. Again, carefully lift and turn the sheet
over. Cut two small pieces from the drinking straw
and stick one at the end of each length of tape.

*Strips are
neat and flat*

LORD OF THE RINGS

Saturn's magnificent rings make this planet one of the wonders of the solar system. They stretch 300,000 miles (480,000 km) from Saturn's cloud tops, and the faint, outermost ring is farther from Saturn than the Moon is from Earth. Though vast in width, the rings are only a few dozen yards thick and seem to disappear when seen edge-on. They are made of billions of sparkling fragments of rock and ice, ranging in size from dust particles to enormous boulders over half a mile across. The fragments are thought to be debris from a catastrophic collision, perhaps between a moon and a comet.

Rings within rings ▲
Space probes have shown Saturn's rings to be made of thousands of smaller ringlets. The gaps between the rings are cleared by gravity from nearby moons.

HANDY TIP
Roll the two straws slowly over the tape at the same time using equal speed and pressure.

Squeeze firmly to secure everything in place

3 **Pass a bamboo skewer** through the straws. Now, carefully roll the tape around the straws, taking care not to let the paper strips get bunched up and stick it down.

4 **Tie a long elastic band on** to the metal ring and attach it to both the skewer and the top of the device with a blob of Plasticine.

5 **Loop the elastic band** over a pencil. Twirl the device around to twist the band, then release to let it spin.

Make sure the bottom can move freely up and down the skewer

Shooting stars

When specks of rock debris hit Earth's atmosphere and burn up, they make streaks of light called shooting stars. You can see shooting stars every clear night, but they are more common at certain times of year when they fall in "meteor showers." Most shooting stars are caused by debris the size of sand, but occasional apple-sized rocks produce fantastic fireballs with long tails.

1 **Choose a clear, moonless night** and a dark location far from city lights to see the most shooting stars. It's best to watch after midnight, when Earth's night side faces incoming space debris head-on, producing faster and brighter shooting stars. You should see a shooting star about every 15 minutes or so.

2 **Take a folding chair** and make sure you're comfortable. The two biggest challenges for a shooting-star spotter are cold and patience. To keep you occupied, use a constellation guide and try to identify as many constellations as possible, or watch for shooting stars with a friend or parent. To keep you warm while you're waiting, wear lots of clothes and take a sleeping bag.

SPECTACULAR COMETS

Comets are gigantic balls of ice and dust that occasionally swoop through the inner solar system and become visible from Earth. As a comet approaches the Sun, its icy surface warms up and evaporates, releasing a glowing tail of gas and dust. When Earth passes through the trail of dust left by a comet, the dust particles cause meteor showers.

◄ **A comet's tails**
Comet Hale-Bopp passed Earth in 1997 with a blue and a white tail. The tails of a comet point away from the Sun, whichever way it flies.

- Folding chair or recliner
- Photocopy of your constellation chart to sketch on
- Warm clothes
- Sleeping bag
- Notepad and pen

Never go out alone at night — ask an adult to come along, too. Dress up warmly.

METEOR SHOWERS

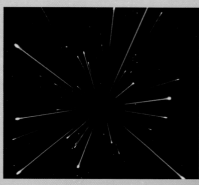

A shower of meteors

During a meteor shower you might see dozens of shooting stars an hour. On rare occasions, the rate goes up to thousands an hour—a "meteor storm." Meteor showers happen at the same time each year, when Earth's orbit crosses the dust trail of a comet. The paths of the meteors are in fact parallel, but appear to radiate out from a single point because of their position and distance from Earth.

Warm clothes are essential when you're watching shooting stars, even in summer

HANDY TIP

A fully reclining lounger makes it even more comfortable to skywatch for long periods.

3 During a meteor shower, shooting stars all appear to come from the same point in the sky—the radiant. Most meteor showers are named after the constellation in which the radiant is located. Try to work out where the radiant is by sketching each shooting star on a photocopied star chart (see pages 46–47). Make a note of the size and color of each shooting star.

Dial the stars

One of the most useful pieces of equipment a stargazer can have is a planisphere. With this simple device, you can find out exactly what stars you're looking at on any night, at any time. You can buy a planisphere, but you can also make one. It has two parts: a base showing a star chart and a rotating mask with an oval window.

WHAT YOU WILL NEED

- Access to a photocopier or color scanner, computer, and printer
- Glue
- Posterboard
- Scissors
- Atlas
- Sheet of stiff, clear plastic
- Paper fastener
- Compass

Selecting the time and date

The numbers around the edge of the mask show the time of day. Turn the mask around until the time lines up with the date. The window now shows all the visible constellations. Remember that the stars in the sky will appear much smaller and more spread out than on the planisphere.

Mask

Clear plastic

Star chart

Posterboard

The layers of the planisphere

Paper fastener

1 **Photocopy the mask** in color, if you can, along with the appropriate star chart (see pages 46–47); use an enlargement factor of 200 percent. Or, scan them onto a computer and print them in color at double size. Glue the paper to some posterboard and trim both with scissors.

Choosing the correct mask

Check your latitude in an atlas and cut out the mask that is closest.

Selecting the correct time

Use white numbers for the time in the Northern Hemisphere; black numbers for the Southern Hemisphere.

35°
42°
52°

N
W — E
S
Southern Hemisphere

S
E — W
N
Northern Hemisphere

Planisphere mask

Using your planisphere

Once you've lined up the time and date (see left), use a compass to check that North or South is right and hold the planisphere above your head. Try to match constellations in the sky to those on the planisphere. It's tricky at first but becomes easier with practice.

2 **Check your latitude** in an atlas and cut out the relevant oval on the mask. Stick your mask to some clear plastic and trim the plastic to match the size of the star chart.

3 **Push a hole** through the middle (carefully using closed scissors) and attach both layers with a paper fastener so that the disks can turn freely.

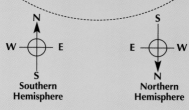

Star charts

These charts show the brightest stars visible to the naked eye on a clear night. There are two charts: one centered on the north celestial pole, and one on the south celestial pole (there is overlap). You can see only half the sky at any time. To find out which stars are visible on a particular night, use a chart to make a planisphere (see pages 44–45).

Constellations

The labels and yellow lines on the charts show the patterns of stars that astronomers call constellations. On an average night, you'll see only the brightest stars, so don't worry if you find it difficult to recognize many constellations. It does get easier with practice.

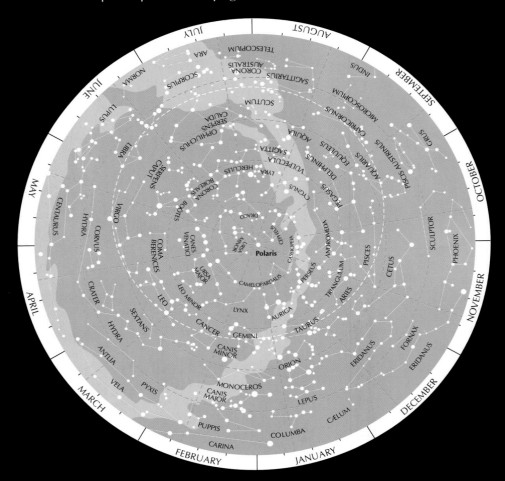

Northern Hemisphere constellations

READING THE CHARTS

Orion with Sirius showing just above the horizon

Star charts can be confusing when you start using them. Because they show the whole dome of the night sky in a small area, the stars look much closer together than they really are. The charts also seem to show that some stars are bigger than others, but in fact they are really showing the stars' brightness, or "magnitude." The large dots represent the brightest stars, which are easiest to see. Small dots are faint stars, which are visible only on the darkest, clearest nights. Astronomers use a scale of numbers for magnitude. The scale goes backward, so large numbers represent faint stars. The naked eye can see stars down to a magnitude of 6. Sirius, the brightest star in the sky, has a magnitude of –1.4, and a full Moon can reach –13.

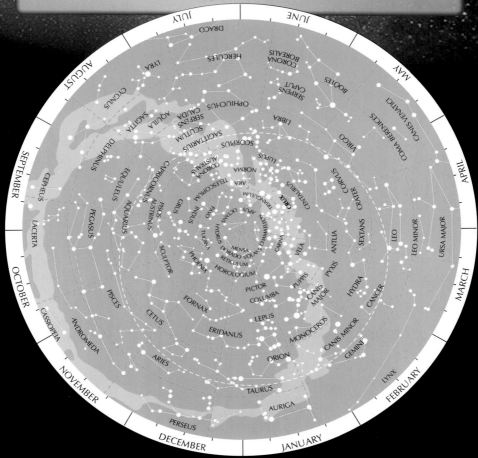

Southern Hemisphere constellations

Compass stars

Because Earth is spinning around, the stars appear to rotate around the night sky. But there are two points that never move—the north and south celestial poles. These are always at the same points in the sky, due north and due south. Once you know how to find a celestial pole, you can use it as a compass to find your way.

Star trails

If you take a long-exposure photograph of the night sky, the stars' movement across it will create circles of light called "star trails." As well as showing the apparent movement of stars (actually caused by Earth's rotation), star trails reveal the stars' different colors. The central star in this picture is Polaris (the Pole Star), which is about 1° away from the true celestial pole, so it makes a short but bright streak.

FIND THE NORTH CELESTIAL POLE

If you live in the Northern Hemisphere, you can see the north celestial pole, but not the southern one. Finding the north celestial pole is fairly easy because there's a star that almost exactly marks the spot: the Pole Star, Polaris.

1 **To find Polaris**, first locate the Big Dipper—one of the brightest groups of stars. It's always visible in the Northern Hemisphere (if you live at latitude 40° or more), though it's much lower in the night sky in fall than in spring, when it's overhead at midnight.

2 **Draw an imaginary line** from the Big Dipper between the last two stars (the "Pointers") and extend it five times the distance between the stars to take you to Polaris. Measuring three hand-widths from the Pointers will also take you to Polaris. If you face Polaris (due north), you can work out all directions.

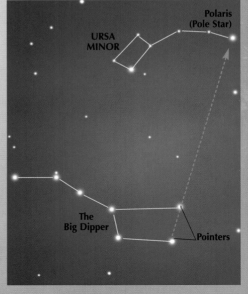

URSA MINOR

Polaris (Pole Star)

The Big Dipper

Pointers

FIND THE SOUTH CELESTIAL POLE

For people who live in the Southern Hemisphere, the south celestial pole is always above the horizon at the same point, due south. However, it's trickier to find than the north celestial pole because there are no stars in it—it's just a blank area of sky.

Southern Cross

Southern Pointers

South celestial pole

1 **First, locate the Southern Cross,** a distinctive constellation in the southern sky. Like the Big Dipper, the Southern Cross is visible throughout the year because it's close to the pole. The easiest way to find it is to look for two exceptionally bright stars nearby, called the Southern Pointers, which point to the Southern Cross.

2 **Draw an imaginary line** from the base of the Southern Cross (the star Acrux). Extend it by about five times the "height" of the cross, or three hand-widths, to take you to the south celestial pole. You could also imagine a straight line at right angles to the Pointers. The pole lies where this line intersects the line from the cross.

Northern star-hopping

If you live in the Northern Hemisphere, you can use the Big Dipper and Polaris (the Pole Star) as stepping stones to find other stars. Try finding some of the constellations near Polaris, which are in the sky year-round. You will need a clear, dark night to see them all, since some are faint.

The lozenge

DRACO

URSA MINOR

M81 galaxy

URSA MAJOR
(The Big Dipper)

The Pointers

1 **First, find the Big Dipper** and locate the "Pointers"— the last two stars in the bowl of the dipper. Draw an imaginary line **(a)** from the Pointers and extend it to the Pole Star, Polaris. Polaris is in the faint constellation Ursa Minor, which you can see only on clear, dark nights.

2 **Extend the line** a little way past Polaris to find the faint constellation Cepheus, which looks like a lopsided house. If you have binoculars, sweep the area around the base of the "house." You'll see a very red star—the Garnet Star. This is the reddest star visible to the naked eye and the largest star yet discovered.

3 **Draw a new line (b)** to Polaris from the third star in the Big Dipper's handle, and then to a bright constellation that looks like a flattened letter W. This is Cassiopeia. You can use the positions of the Big Dipper and Cassiopeia to tell time (see pages 54–55).

Garnet star

Delta Cephei

CEPHEUS

M52 star
cluster

CASSIOPEIA

NGC 457
star cluster

Polaris

*The hazy cloud of
the Milky Way –
our own galaxy*

4 **The next constellation** is faint
and tricky to see, so look for it
only if the sky is very dark. Draw a line
(c) starting from the fourth star in the Big
Dipper's handle (as shown) to a long,
winding constellation called Draco.
Four stars make up the dragon's head—
a pattern of stars called the "lozenge."

5 **Use some binoculars** to try to find
a galaxy. Return to the area around
the Big Dipper and look for a pair of tiny
fuzzy patches (shown here by two brown
ovals). These are galaxies. The brighter one
is a beautiful spiral galaxy called M81.

POLAR CONSTELLATIONS

◄ Ursa Minor
Also known as the Little
Bear, this faint constellation
looks like a miniature version
of the Big Dipper. Its
brightest star is Polaris, which has been used
for centuries as an aid to navigation. Sailors
used to call Polaris "Stella Maris," which
means "star of the sea."

Ursa Major ►
The seven stars of the Big
Dipper make up the tail
and rump of the Great
Bear, or Ursa Major, as
it's officially known.
One of its most
interesting "stars" is the second star along
the handle of the dipper. If you look closely
and have sharp eyes, you will see it's
actually a double star.

◄ Cassiopeia
The ancient Greeks named
this constellation after a vain
queen, and pictured her on
a throne, admiring herself in
a mirror. Cassiopeia lies in the
band of the Milky Way. Sweep
this area with binoculars to
see if you can see several
star clusters around it.

Cepheus ►
In Greek mythology,
Cepheus was married to
Cassiopeia. An interesting
star in this constellation is
Delta Cephei, which is a
"variable star." Variable stars
pulse in size and brightness.
Delta Cephei has a 5-day cycle,
so you can watch it change
with binoculars over successive nights.

◄ Draco
Draco means "dragon"—an
apt name for a constellation
that snakes across the night
sky. If you've got some
good binoculars and a clear,
dark night, then sweep the area along the
dragon's tail to see if you can find any
double stars. Don't worry if you can't
make any out—many stars in Draco are
quite faint.

Southern star-hopping

Stargazers who live in the Southern Hemisphere don't have the advantage of a pole star to help them hop around the night sky. But they can see far more bright stars in the polar region, as well as colorful nebulas, galaxies, and star-packed parts of our own galaxy—the Milky Way. Crux and the Southern Pointers are the starting points for a hop around the southern sky.

1 **First, locate the Southern Cross** and Southern Pointers (Alpha and Beta Centauri). Draw a line **(a)** from Beta Centauri through the bottom of the Southern Cross and extend it by the same distance again. You'll reach a red cloud in the constellation Carina—the Eta Carinae nebula (shown as a red square). Take a closer look at this fabulous sight with binoculars. Deep inside is a massive star (Eta Carinae) that is likely to explode in the distant future.

2 **Close to the nebula** are two beautiful star clusters—NGC 3532 (shown as orange dots) and the Southern Pleiades. Through binoculars they look like sparkling jewels. Look at the Southern Pleiades without binoculars and count the stars. You'll find you can count more stars when you look slightly to one side of it.

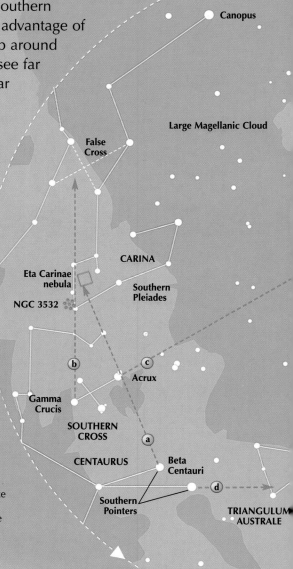

Canopus

Large Magellanic Cloud

False Cross

CARINA

Eta Carinae nebula

NGC 3532

Southern Pleiades

b

c

Acrux

Gamma Crucis

SOUTHERN CROSS

a

CENTAURUS

Beta Centauri

Southern Pointers

d

TRIANGULUM AUSTRALE

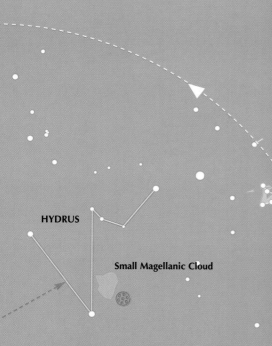

HYDRUS

Small Magellanic Cloud

3 **Now, draw a line (b)** from the top of the Southern Cross, past the Eta Carinae nebula, and onward by the same distance again. This takes you to what looks like another cross—the "false cross," which often confuses stargazers. Just beyond it is star cluster IC 2391, which is worthy of closer inspection with binoculars.

4 **Draw the next line (c)** continuing the long bar of the Southern Cross straight out across the empty part of the sky to a small, fuzzy cloud— the Small Magellanic Cloud (see also page 67). This cloud is a small galaxy, 200,000 light-years from Earth. Through binoculars, you can see nebulas and star clusters within it. Nearby is the second-best globular cluster (a dense ball of very ancient stars) in the night sky, called 47 Tucanae.

5 **Finally, return** to the Southern Pointers and draw a line **(d)** from Alpha Centauri to discover three bright stars in a triangle shape. This is the constellation Triangulum Australe.

POLAR CONSTELLATIONS

Southern Cross (Crux) ▶
The Southern Cross is in the main band of the Milky Way. Near its base is a dark patch in the Milky Way—a dust cloud called the Coalsack. The foot of the Cross is the star Acrux (in fact a double star). The top is a red giant called Gamma Crucis.

◀ Centaurus
The Southern Pointers are part of the constellation Centaurus, which is said to resemble the mythical beast called a centaur, a creature half-man and half-horse. Alpha Centauri is the third-brightest star in the sky and the closest star that's visible to the naked eye, at only 4.4 light-years away from Earth.

Carina ▶
The constellation Carina contains the brightest nebula in the night sky (the Eta Carinae nebula). From the Greek for the "keel" of a boat, Carina stretches across to brilliant Canopus, the second-brightest star in the sky. Canopus is 15,000 times brighter than the Sun, but is so far away that it doesn't blind us.

◀ Hydrus
The faint constellation Hydrus— which means water snake—is very close to the Small Magellanic Cloud. Like many southern constellations, Hydrus was named relatively recently by European explorers when they sailed the southern seas. With good binoculars, you can see a pair of red giant stars in the middle of Hydrus.

Triangulum Australe ▶
The three bright stars of Triangulum Australe stand out strongly against the hazy background of the Milky Way, in which this constellation lies. Triangulum Australe—or Southern Triangle—was named by European explorers in the sixteenth century. Sweep the area around it with binoculars to see if you can find the star cluster NGC 6025.

The time at night

Whether you live in the Southern or the Northern Hemisphere, you can use the stars to tell the time. Make this star clock and learn how to use it to the amazement of your friends. You'll need to know how to find the celestial pole (see pages 48–49).

The Big Dipper

WHAT YOU WILL NEED

- Access to a photocopier or scanner and printer
- Paper or posterboard
- Glue
- Scissors
- Paper fastener

Using your clock

Hold the star clock vertically in front of you. Turn it so that the date is at the top. Keep the base disk still and turn the top disk on the front until the constellations match their positions in the sky. Read off the time from the small hole.

The Big Dipper

Northern Hemisphere—base disk

DECEMBER JANUARY FEBRUARY MARCH APRIL MAY JUNE JULY AUGUST SEPTEMBER OCTOBER NOVEMBER

24 23 22 21 20 19 18 17 16 15 14 13 12 11 10 9 8 7 6 5 4 3 2 1

TIME

Cassiopeia   Pole Star   The Big Dipper

Instructions

Face due north, using the Pole Star to work out where north is. Hold the star clock vertically in front of you. Turn it so that the date is at the top. Keep the base disk still and turn the top disk on the front until the constellations match their position in the sky. Read off the time from the small hole.

Northern Hemisphere—top disk

1 **If you live** in the Northern Hemisphere, use the two disks on this page. If you live in the Southern Hemisphere, use the two disks on the right. Photocopy them onto stiff paper, or photocopy them onto regular paper and glue the larger disk to a posterboard circle. Alternatively, scan them into a computer and print on stiff paper.

TWENTY-FOUR HOURS

The 24-hour clock can be traced back to ancient Egyptian stargazers. From paintings on coffins up to 4,000 years old, we know they used the sky as a clock. They watched for certain stars to rise at intervals through the night. On average, 12 of their chosen stars came up between sunset and sunrise, so they divided the night into 12 periods. About 2,000 years ago, the Greek astronomer Hipparchus first suggested dividing a whole day and night into 24 equal hours.

▲ **Clock watching**
Ancient Egyptians watching the clock stars using an alignment device called a Merkhet.

Turn the top disk but keep the bottom disk still

Southern Hemisphere—base disk

Instructions
Face due south, using the Southern Cross and Southern Pointers to work out where the south celestial pole is. Hold the star clock vertically in front of you. Turn it so that the date is at the top. Keep the base disk still and turn the top disk on the front until the constellations match their position in the sky. Read off the time from the small hole.

TIME

Celestial pole

Southern Pointers

Southern Cross

Achernar

Canopus

Southern Hemisphere—top disk

② **Carefully cut out** the two disks. Place the smaller disk on the center of the large disk, punch a hole through the center of both, and fix them together with a paper fastener.

Latitude locator

Before the days of satellites and accurate maps, sailors and explorers used the stars to find their way. The stars not only told them which way was north, but also told them their latitude—how far they were from Earth's equator. The device they used to work out their latitude was a quadrant, a simple viewing device that you can make yourself. As well as using a quadrant to work out your latitude, you can use it to measure the angle (altitude) of stars and planets above the horizon.

WHAT YOU WILL NEED

- Compass
- Posterboard
- Pen
- Protractor
- Scissors
- Paper
- Adhesive tape
- String
- Large heavy washer or similar weight

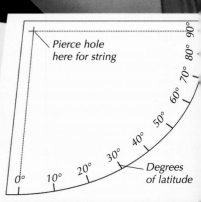

LOCATION LOCATION LOCATION

You can specify your location anywhere on Earth with two numbers: longitude and latitude. Longitude divides the world into 360 sections from pole to pole, like segments of an orange. Lines of latitude run East to West and show you how far you are from the equator. To understand latitude, imagine standing on the North Pole, where the Pole Star is always overhead. If you point at it, your arm will be at 90° to the ground—the North Pole's latitude is 90°. Now, imagine you're at the equator. The Pole Star is on the horizon, so your outstretched arm makes an angle of 0°.

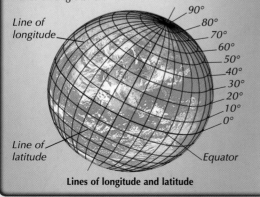

Line of longitude

90°
80°
70°
60°
50°
40°
30°
20°
10°
0°

Line of latitude

Equator

Lines of longitude and latitude

Pierce hole here for string

90°
80°
70°
60°
50°
40°
30°
20°
10°
0°

Degrees of latitude

Labels on quadrant scale:
90°, 80°, 70°, 60°, 50°, 40°, 30°, 0°

Using your quadrant

If you live in the Northern Hemisphere, find the Pole Star (see page 48). Look through the tube at the Pole Star, let the weight settle, then grip it. Look where the string falls to read off your latitude. If you live in the Southern Hemisphere, finding latitude is easiest when the Southern Cross (see page 49) is upright or upside-down. Look through the tube at Acrux, the base of the Southern Cross. If the Cross is upright, subtract 27° from your quadrant's reading; if it is upside-down, add 27°.

HANDY TIP

If you can, rest your elbow on a surface to steady both your view and the weight.

Roll stiff paper around a pen and tape closed

1 **Draw a quarter circle** on posterboard, cut it out, and use a protractor to mark a scale of degrees around the curved edge, running from 0° to 90°. Leave a border of about ½ in (1 cm) on either side of the scale (don't put 0° and 90° right at the edges).

2 **Make a hole** in the corner, taking care to align it perfectly to both the 0° and the 90° gradations. Tie a piece of string, which is attached to a weight, through the hole.

3 **Make the viewing tube** by rolling a piece of paper around a pen. Tape the tube to the 90° side of the quadrant, taking care to make it perfectly straight.

A star is born

New stars are born inside vast, gas clouds
called nebulas, that lie between the stars. One
of the most spectacular nebulas you can see is
the Orion Nebula, which is visible from the
Northern and the Southern Hemispheres.

1 **The best time to see** the Orion Nebula,
which is in the constellation of Orion, is
from December to February, when it's high in
the night sky. If you live in the Northern
Hemisphere, look south. If you live in the
Southern Hemisphere, look north.

The Orion constellation

Horsehead
Nebula

Alnitak

Orion Nebula

2 **When you've spotted** the distinctive
shape of Orion, look for the three stars
that make up Orion's "belt." Hanging from
the belt is Orion's "sword," in the middle of
which is the Orion Nebula. You can see the
nebula with the naked eye, but binoculars
will reveal more detail. Deep inside this
cloud, new stars are forming. Photographs of
the Orion Nebula reveal glorious colors.
Unfortunately, you can't see these colors with
the naked eye or binoculars.

3 **Look again at the star** in the center of
the Orion Nebula. With the naked eye
you can see one star, but with binoculars you
might see two. In fact, there's a group of at
least four newly-formed stars called the
Trapezium, after their shape, right in the heart
of the nebula. The energy emitted by these
new stars is making the gas in the nebula glow.

Orion the Hunter

Orion is named after a hunter in Greek myths. Southern Hemisphere viewers see the hunter upside-down, with his feet at the top and shoulders at the bottom.

Horsehead Nebula

4 **If you had** a powerful telescope, you could search for another interesting nebula in Orion, shown in the picture above. It's called the Horsehead Nebula, because of its shape. It is actually a dark cloud of dust silhouetted against the red gas cloud behind it. The Horsehead Nebula is just below Alnitak, the left star in Orion's belt.

STARBIRTH NEBULAS

Stars form when the force of gravity makes pockets of gas in nebulas shrink. Exactly the same process gave birth to our Sun (see page 11). The gas in most starbirth nebulas is too faint to see, even with binoculars. However, cameras can capture the hazy colors with breathtaking results.

North America Nebula ▶
This curious nebula in the constellation Cygnus looks like a map of North America, complete with its own Gulf of Mexico. The nebula is lit up by the newly formed stars within it.

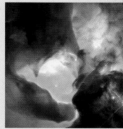

Lagoon Nebula ▶
The Lagoon Nebula is in the constellation Sagittarius and is easy to see with the naked eye, or via binoculars. This close-up image from the Hubble telescope shows twisted columns of gas and a new star.

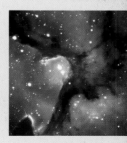

Trifid Nebula ▶
This nebula is also in Sagittarius. You can just see it with binoculars, but you need a good telescope to see any level of detail. The dark bands crossing the nebula are lanes of dust that block the light.

Columns in the Eagle Nebula ▶
These colossal pillars of hydrogen gas were also photographed by the Hubble telescope. New stars are forming in the "fingers" of gas at the top of the biggest pillar. The fingers are bigger than our solar system.

Find the Seven Sisters

The Seven Sisters is the common name for a star cluster called the Pleiades. Oddly, nobody actually sees seven stars in the Pleiades – most people see six. Good eyesight, or using binoculars, actually reveals more than seven.

When to look

If you live in the Northern Hemisphere, the best time to see the Pleiades is in fall or winter. The best Southern Hemisphere views are in spring and summer. The cluster reaches its highest point in the sky at midnight in November. The image on the right is a highly magnified view.

WHAT YOU WILL NEED

- No equipment essential, but binoculars and a planisphere are useful

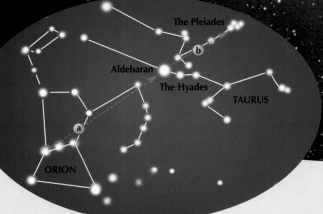

1 First, locate Orion and its belt. (To find out more about Orion, look on pages 58–59). In the Northern Hemisphere, you should draw an imaginary line (a) up through Orion's belt, past the shoulder of Orion, and onward to a bright, reddish star called Aldebaran, which is part of the constellation Taurus. If you live in the Southern Hemisphere, where Orion is upside-down, draw the line down from his belt and then on to Aldebaran.

2 If you have binoculars, take a close look at Aldebaran, a red giant star that varies slightly in brightness. (Find out about red giants on pages 62–63.) Next to Aldebaran, you can see an open star cluster (see box right) called the Hyades.

3 Now, hop beyond Aldebaran, traveling away from Orion in roughly the same direction but for a slightly shorter distance (b). You'll come to the Pleiades star cluster—one of the most beautiful sights in the night sky.

The starlight from the Pleiades takes about 400 years to reach Earth

STAR CLUSTERS

Double star cluster in LMC NGC 1850

Tightly packed groups of stars are called star clusters, and there are two main types. Open clusters, such as the Hyades and the Pleiades, are loose groups of young, hot stars that glow with a bluish brilliance. Globular clusters, on the other hand, are dense balls of hundreds of thousands of very ancient stars. Unlike open clusters, which lie within the Milky Way galaxy, globular clusters are often above or below the galaxy's plane. One of the most spectacular is Omega Centauri in the constellation Centaurus, which is visible from the Southern Hemisphere. The most impressive globular cluster visible to northern viewers is the Hercules Cluster, in the Hercules constellation.

HANDY TIP

Do not look for faint objects during a full moon, because the moonlight is too bright.

4 **Take a good look** at the Pleiades with the naked eye. How many stars can you count? If you have binoculars, look again. Can you count more? There are actually more than 3,000 stars in the Pleiades. At only 78 million years old, these stars are babies in astronomical terms, and wouldn't have been in the night sky during the age of the dinosaurs. With a powerful telescope you can see a blue haze around the stars, which is a dust cloud through which the stars are currently passing.

Going, going, gone

All stars eventually run out of energy
and die. As they grow older, their
surface cools down and turns red. Stars
also swell in size with age, becoming
"red giants" and "red supergiants." Such
stars are easy to spot, and their warm
color is obvious even to the naked eye.

If Betelgeuse blew up

Betelgeuse is a red supergiant in Orion. Astronomers
think it's near the end of its life and is about to blow
apart, in a colossal explosion called a supernova.
The artist's impression on the right shows what a
Betelgeuse supernova might look like from Earth.
For a few weeks, the star would outshine the Moon
and cast shadows on Earth.

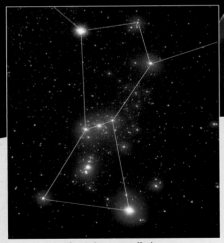

The Orion constellation

Red stars	**Orange stars**	**Yellow stars**
5,400°F	7,200°F	10,800°F
(3,000°C)	(4,000°C)	(6,000°C)
White stars	**Light-blue stars**	**Blue stars**
18,000°F	36,000°F	90,000°F
(10,000°C)	(20,000°C)	(50,000°C)

1 **One of the easiest** red supergiants to see
is Betelgeuse, on the left shoulder of Orion
(as we look at it). Betelgeuse is about
800 times wider than our Sun. Look at
Betelgeuse with binoculars, and compare its
color to the blue supergiant Rigel—the very
bright star in the opposite corner of Orion
(the right foot). Blue supergiants form when red
supergiants lose some of their outer atmosphere.
They can also explode as supernovas.

2 **You can tell** a star's surface temperature from
its color. Blue stars are hottest, red are coolest.
Use the guide above to work out the temperature of
these stars: Rigel, Vega (the brightest star in Lyra),
Arcturus (brightest star in Boötes), Capella (brightest
star in Auriga), Sirius (brightest star in Canis Major),
and Deneb (brightest star in Cygnus).

WHEN STARS DIE

What happens when a star dies depends on its weight. Light stars swell into red giants and then throw off their outer layers into space, forming ghostly clouds called planetary nebulas, leaving behind a small star called a white dwarf. Massive stars swell into much bigger red supergiants. When they finally run out of energy to resist the awesome inward pull of their own gravity, they collapse in an instant. The collapse creates a devastating shock wave that hurls out the star's outer layers in an explosion brighter than a billion suns, called a supernova. The dense core may then survive as a "neutron star." But the most massive cores continue to shrink under their gravity until they are smaller than an atom. The result is a black hole—a gravitational trap from which nothing can escape.

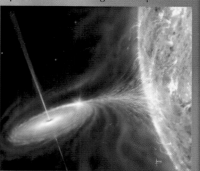

Black holes ▲
This artist's impression shows a black hole (left) sucking in a spinning cloud of matter from a neighboring blue giant star (right).

Awesome Antares

During the summer, look for the red supergiant Antares, the brightest star in Scorpius. Antares is one of the reddest stars in the sky (it's name means "anti-Ares" or the "Rival of Mars," a reflection of the red color of both objects). It's almost as bright as Betelgeuse and about 620,000 miles (1 million km) wide, making it 700 times wide

The red supergiant Antares (far left)

Our local galaxy

Almost every star you can see in the night sky belongs to the Milky Way – our local galaxy. The Milky Way is a gargantuan, spinning whirlpool of 200 billion stars, most of which are clustered in the center, or spread along spiral arms. On dark, clear nights, you can sometimes see it stretching across the sky as a hazy band.

Spiral arms curve out from the heart of galaxy NGC 1232

Distorting dust

Dust clouds in some parts of the Milky Way block out the light from the stars beyond, creating dark lanes in our view of the galaxy. In the picture above, dark clouds of dust have mixed with glowing gas clouds, creating a multicolored spectacle.

From a distance

If you could see the Milky Way from a great distance, it might look like the spiral galaxy NGC 1232. Because we're inside the Milky Way, we see it side-on and can't see its spiral shape. If there were no dust clouds in the way, we might get a view like the one below. This image shows the galaxy's flat shape and central bulge, where stars are packed most densely. From side to side, the whole Milky Way measures about 600 million billion miles (1 billion billion km).

Galaxy NGC 1232

Our solar system is in one of the spiral arms about halfway from the center

The Milky Way viewed side-on from space

Viewing the Milky Way

To see the Milky Way in all its glory,
you need a clear, moonless night, free of light
pollution. Parts of the Milky Way are visible for
much of the year, but to see the best areas you need to
know when and where to look. Northern Hemisphere
viewers should look at the constellations Cygnus and
Aquila in late summer. In the Southern Hemisphere, you
should look at Sagittarius and Scorpius in winter for a
stunning view of the galaxy's star-packed center.

GALAXY IN A CUP

You can make a model of the Milky Way with
everyday ingredients, such as coffee and cream. Ask
an adult to make a cup of black coffee for you. Stir
the coffee quite quickly to make it spin, then gently
lower in a spoonful of cream. The cream will form
a spinning spiral. In reality, the Milky Way spins in
a very different way from cream in a coffee cup.
The spiral arms don't rotate as whole objects –
they are simply places where stars get temporarily
crowded during their journey around the galaxy,
like cars passing through a traffic jam.

A homemade spiral galaxy ▶

Galaxy hunting

If you know where to look, you can see far beyond our local galaxy. Spot three of the Milky Way's closest neighbors, including its two satellite galaxies, and the most distant object visible to the human eye.

Andromeda galaxy

The Andromeda galaxy is the most distant object the naked eye can see. It's about 2.5 million light-years away, which means we see it as it was 2.5 million years ago, before humans had even evolved. It's a spiral galaxy, like the Milky Way, but one-and-a-half times the size, with 400 billion stars. Close to it are two small companion galaxies, one of which (M32) is visible in this picture as a fuzzy white spot.

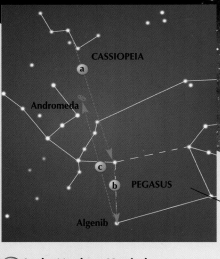

CASSIOPEIA

a

Andromeda

c

b PEGASUS

Algenib

On good nights you might see ten stars in the Great Square of Pegasus; on poor nights it appears empty.

1 **In the Northern Hemisphere**, the only external galaxy you can see with the unaided eye is the Andromeda Galaxy. To "star hop" to it, start with the "W"-shaped constellation Cassiopeia (see pages 50–51). Draw a line **(a)** from the middle star in Cassiopeia, through the star at the deepest point in the W, and on to a bright star at the corner of a large square. The square is part of the constellation Pegasus, which is named after a mythological winged horse.

2 Now, "hop" counterclockwise **(b)** around the Great Square of Pegasus to the next star, Algenib. Draw a line **(c)** from Algenib back up to Cassiopeia. Just over halfway along is a blurry oval—the Andromeda galaxy. The galaxy is visible to the naked eye in good conditions, and binoculars will reveal the galaxy's bright center. With a big telescope, the spiral arms are visible, too. With good binoculars you might just be able to see one of the Andromeda galaxy's small companion galaxies, known as M32.

Large Magellanic Cloud

This galaxy is one of our closest neighbors, 170,000 light-years away. It orbits the Milky Way as a satellite and is only a fraction of the size of the Milky Way. The Large and Small Magellanic Clouds are named after the Portuguese explorer, Ferdinand Magellan, who saw them on the first round-the-world sailing trip.

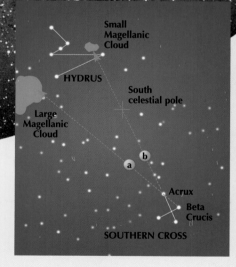

WHAT YOU WILL NEED

- **No equipment essential, but binoculars and a planisphere are useful**

1 **Stargazers in the** Southern Hemisphere can see the Milky Way's companion galaxies, the Large and Small Magellanic Clouds. From the far south, these can be seen in the sky all year round. To locate the Large Magellanic Cloud, start from the Southern Cross. Draw a line (a) from Beta Crucis through Acrux, and extend it until you reach a cloudy patch—this is the Large Magellanic Cloud. Using binoculars, you might be able to see star clusters and nebulas within this galaxy. The largest nebula is the Tarantula Nebula.

2 **To find the** Small Magellanic Cloud, draw a line (b) down the long shaft of the Southern Cross and extend it to another cloudy patch near the Hydrus constellation. Binoculars may help to reveal star clusters and nebulas within it.

Expanding universe

The universe is everything—planets, stars,
galaxies, and all the nothingness in
between. Astronomers have discovered
that the universe is getting bigger,
but could it keep growing forever?
It is difficult for the mind to
picture, but this simple activity
with a balloon can help you to
understand this expansion.

Ballooning out
The universe isn't expanding "into" anything
because there's no space outside it and no
outer edge. Imagine that the galaxies are on
the surface of a balloon. Like the universe, the
balloon's surface has no center and no outer
boundary, yet it can still expand.

THE ACCELERATING UNIVERSE

Hubble Telescope image of remote galaxies and stars

When astronomers point their most powerful telescopes at
tiny areas of the sky, they get pictures like the one above. It
shows galaxies stretching into the distance as far as we can
see, each one home to billions of stars and planets. Careful
observations show that all the galaxies are getting farther
apart, so the whole universe must be expanding. Oddly, the
expansion is speeding up, yet the force of gravity ought to
slow it down. Astronomers think the universe must therefore
be full of an invisible force called "dark energy" that is
somehow repelling gravity and pushing everything apart. The
same force may have played a role in the Big Bang.

WHAT YOU WILL NEED

- Balloons
- Permanent marker pen

1 **Use a permanent**
marker pen to draw
galaxies on a balloon. If you find
it easier, you can do this after
you have first inflated it a little.

THE BIG BANG

When the universe began

The universe began 13 billion years ago, when it exploded out of nothingness. In a second, it grew from being tinier than an atom to 125 million billion miles (200 million billion km) wide. It has been expanding ever since and may do so forever. Some scientists think time itself began in the Big Bang, but that may always remain a mystery.

*Draw spirals
to represent
galaxies*

(2) **Blow up the balloon** and tie the end. The galaxies have become much larger and spread farther apart. The galaxies in the real universe are also getting farther apart, but they're not growing in size.

*The galaxies
move apart as
the balloon
expands*

Glossary

Asteroid Any of numerous, small celestial bodies, made of rock, metal, or both, in solar orbit. Most asteroid orbits lie between Mars and Jupiter.

Astronomy The scientific study of space.

Atmosphere The layer of gas trapped around a planet by the force of gravity.

Atom The smallest unit of matter, which cannot be divided into smaller parts, except in a nuclear reaction.

Axis An imaginary line that passes through the center of a planet, or other body, and around which the body rotates.

Big Bang The violent explosion that gave birth to the universe 13 billion years ago.

Billion A number equivalent to one thousand million.

Black hole A point in space with such a powerful gravitational pull that nothing, not even light, can escape.

Celestial pole The point at the top or bottom of the celestial sphere. The north and south celestial poles do not move during the night and are always due north or due south.

Celestial sphere This imaginary globe surrounds Earth. Stars move around Earth as if fixed points on this sphere.

Circumpolar star A star that does not set, but remains above the horizon, and circles the celestial pole.

Comet A body made of ice and rocky dust. When a comet nears the Sun, its surface evaporates and releases gas and dust in glowing tails.

Constellation A pattern of stars in the sky, often named after a mythological person or creature.

Core The innermost part of a star or planet.

Corona The faint upper atmosphere of the Sun, which is visible as a halo only during a total solar eclipse.

Cosmos An alternative name for the universe.

Crater A bowl-shaped depression that can be formed by a meteorite impact or by a volcanic eruption.

Crust The outer, rocky part of a planet or moon.

Dark energy A theoretical force that is thought to be causing the accelerating expansion of the universe. Its true nature is a mystery.

Degree A unit used in measuring angles or distances across a sphere or globe.

Eclipse The effect when the shadow of a moon, or planet, is cast on another celestial body.

Ecliptic The imaginary line around the sky that traces the movement of the Sun through the year.

Ellipse An oval shape. The orbits of planets are ellipses.

Escape velocity The speed at which an object must travel to escape the pull of gravity.

Galaxy A group of millions or billions of stars held together by gravity.

Giant planet A large planet that is made mainly of hydrogen and helium, and is sometimes referred to as a "gas giant" as a consequence. Jupiter, Saturn, Uranus, and Neptune are giant planets.

Globular cluster A dense ball of very ancient stars.

Gravity The invisible force of attraction that exists between all objects.

Greenhouse effect The process by which heat radiated from the ground is trapped by gases in the atmosphere, such as carbon dioxide, leading to global warming.

Hydrogen The most common chemical element in the universe. Hydrogen is the main component of stars and galaxies.

Interstellar A term that means "between the stars."

Latitude A measure of the distance north or south of Earth's equator. Latitude is measured in degrees and shown on globes as lines parallel to the equator.

Light pollution The glow in the sky caused by street lights and atmospheric pollution. Light pollution makes stargazing difficult in cities.

Light-year The unit of astronomical distance based on the distance light travels in a year—6 million million miles (10 million million km).

Longitude The distance measured in degrees around the Earth, east or west, from a line of 0°, which passes through Greenwich in London, England.

Magnitude The brightness of a star. Bright objects have low or negative numbers; faint objects have high numbers.

Mass A measure of the amount of matter in an object. Mass is similar to weight, but objects have weight only when they are on Earth or another large body with significant gravity.

Matter Any material that has mass and occupies space.

Meteor A rock that burns up as it enters Earth's atmosphere, forming a shooting star.

Meteor shower A period when the rate of shooting stars rises as Earth passes through the trail of dust left by a comet.

Meteorite A rock from space that falls to Earth's surface without burning up completely.

Milky Way This is the galaxy in which we live. It can be seen as a pale, milky band across the sky on dark nights.

Moon A large, natural object that orbits a planet.

Naked eye Human vision that is not enhanced in any way.

Nebula A vast cloud of gas and/or dust in space.

Nuclear fusion The joining of the nuclei of atoms. This process releases vast amounts of energy. Nuclear fusion is the energy source of stars.

Observatory A site and equipment used by astronomers to view the sky.

Open cluster A loose cluster of young stars.

Opposition The point in the orbit of a planet when it is on the opposite side of Earth from the Sun, making viewing easy.

Orbit The path in which one object travels around another, more massive, object.

Planet A large, spherical body that orbits a star.

Planetary nebula A cloud of gas and dust puffed out by a dying star.

Planisphere A rotating star chart with a window showing the visible portion of the night sky at particular times and dates, based on your latitude.

Pole Star The star Polaris, which marks the north celestial pole, and around which the sky seems to rotate. The Pole Star is always due north.

Quadrillion A number equivalent to one thousand million million.

Red giant A star, near the end of its life, swollen and reddened as it runs out of nuclear fuel.

Red supergiant A star that has reddened and swollen near the end of its life, before exploding in a supernova.

Rocky planet This type of planet is made largely of rock. Mercury, Venus, Earth, and Mars are all rocky planets.

Satellite An object trapped in orbit around a planet. Moons are natural satellites.

Shooting star Another name for a meteor.

Solar system A sun and its surroundings, including planets and asteroids.

Star A gigantic globe of glowing gas, lit up by nuclear fusion reactions in its core.

Sunspot A relatively cool, dark spot on the Sun's surface.

Supernova A huge explosion when a large star dies.

Trillion A number equivalent to one million million.

Universe Everything that exists—planets, stars, galaxies, and all the space in between.

Variable star A star that varies in brightness. Many variable stars also vary in size.

Void An immense empty region in space.

Zodiac The band of the constellations along the ecliptic. Through the year, the Sun, Moon, and planets appear to move through the constellations of the zodiac.

Index

The author would like to thank **Jon Woodcock** for astronomical expertise.

Model **Jack Williams**

Index **Hilary Bird**

The publisher would like to thank the following for their kind permission to reproduce their photographs:
t = top, b = bottom, l = left, r = right, c = center, a = above
Corbis/Gabe Palmer: 38–9c; NASA/Jet Propulsion Laboratory: 15tr, 20cl, 32bl, 32–3c, 35tr, 36–7, 37tr, b, 39 (Jupiter's moons), 40tl, 41tr; /Marshall Space Flight Center Art Collection: 28l; Science & Society Picture Library: 17tr, 54tr; Science Photo Library/David Nunuk: 4–5, 18tr, 42–3 (background),

44–5 (background), /David A. Hardy: 8bl, 26bl, 63cr, 64b, /Detlev van Ravenswaay: 8–9t, 12, 19t, 56bl, 69tr, /Frank Zullo: 9r, 42bl, 47tl, 64–5 (background), /John Foster: 11bl, /David Ducros: 13tr, 27r, /Mark Garlick: 14bl, 43tr, 68–9, /Cordelia Molloy: 18cl, /Dr Fred Espenak: 18–19b, 24–5t, /John Sanford: 20bl, 20–1 (night sky), 31cl, 56–7 (night sky), 58–59 (background), 62l, /Eckhard Slawik: 20–1 (moon), 23 (moon phases), 54–5 (night sky), /European Southern Observatory: 22tr, 59cl, 64c, /Larry Landolfi: 24bl, 38t, /Dr Juerg Alean: 25b, /NASA: 29tr, 30l, /Pekka Parviainen: 30–1t, 48–9 (background) /NASA/SMU/David P. Anderson: 31cr, /Space Telescope Science Institute/NASA: 33tr, 59cra, 59br, /Rev. Ronald Royer: 39bl, /Jerry

Schad: 46–7 (background), /Tony & Daphne Hallas: 58l, 66–7 (background), /Celestial Image Company: 59tr, 61br, 67t, /National Optical Astronomy Observatories: 59crb, /Royal Observatory, Edinburgh: 60–1 (background), /Luke Dodd: 63b, /MPIA-HD, Birkle, Slawik: 64tl; STScI, Hubble Space Telescope: 5cr, 68b.

All other images © Dorling Kindersley.

For further information see:
www.dkimages.com